AF808191

NAME: ______________________________

PHONE: ______________________________

MOBILE: ______________________________

EMAIL: ______________________________

ADDRESS: ______________________________

A

SITE NAME:	URL:
USERNAME:	PASSWORD:
EMAIL ADDRESS:	
NOTES / SECURITY QUESTIONS:	

SITE NAME:	URL:
USERNAME:	PASSWORD:
EMAIL ADDRESS:	
NOTES / SECURITY QUESTIONS:	

SITE NAME:	URL:
USERNAME:	PASSWORD:
EMAIL ADDRESS:	
NOTES / SECURITY QUESTIONS:	

SITE NAME:	URL:
USERNAME:	PASSWORD:
EMAIL ADDRESS:	
NOTES / SECURITY QUESTIONS:	

A

SITE NAME:	URL:
USERNAME:	PASSWORD:
EMAIL ADDRESS:	
NOTES / SECURITY QUESTIONS:	

SITE NAME:	URL:
USERNAME:	PASSWORD:
EMAIL ADDRESS:	
NOTES / SECURITY QUESTIONS:	

SITE NAME:	URL:
USERNAME:	PASSWORD:
EMAIL ADDRESS:	
NOTES / SECURITY QUESTIONS:	

SITE NAME:	URL:
USERNAME:	PASSWORD:
EMAIL ADDRESS:	
NOTES / SECURITY QUESTIONS:	

A

SITE NAME:	URL:
USERNAME:	PASSWORD:
EMAIL ADDRESS:	
NOTES / SECURITY QUESTIONS:	

SITE NAME:	URL:
USERNAME:	PASSWORD:
EMAIL ADDRESS:	
NOTES / SECURITY QUESTIONS:	

SITE NAME:	URL:
USERNAME:	PASSWORD:
EMAIL ADDRESS:	
NOTES / SECURITY QUESTIONS:	

SITE NAME:	URL:
USERNAME:	PASSWORD:
EMAIL ADDRESS:	
NOTES / SECURITY QUESTIONS:	

A

SITE NAME:	URL:
USERNAME:	PASSWORD:
EMAIL ADDRESS:	
NOTES / SECURITY QUESTIONS:	

SITE NAME:	URL:
USERNAME:	PASSWORD:
EMAIL ADDRESS:	
NOTES / SECURITY QUESTIONS:	

SITE NAME:	URL:
USERNAME:	PASSWORD:
EMAIL ADDRESS:	
NOTES / SECURITY QUESTIONS:	

SITE NAME:	URL:
USERNAME:	PASSWORD:
EMAIL ADDRESS:	
NOTES / SECURITY QUESTIONS:	

B

SITE NAME:	URL:
USERNAME:	PASSWORD:
EMAIL ADDRESS:	
NOTES / SECURITY QUESTIONS:	

SITE NAME:	URL:
USERNAME:	PASSWORD:
EMAIL ADDRESS:	
NOTES / SECURITY QUESTIONS:	

SITE NAME:	URL:
USERNAME:	PASSWORD:
EMAIL ADDRESS:	
NOTES / SECURITY QUESTIONS:	

SITE NAME:	URL:
USERNAME:	PASSWORD:
EMAIL ADDRESS:	
NOTES / SECURITY QUESTIONS:	

B

SITE NAME: | URL:
USERNAME: | PASSWORD:
EMAIL ADDRESS:
NOTES / SECURITY QUESTIONS:

SITE NAME: | URL:
USERNAME: | PASSWORD:
EMAIL ADDRESS:
NOTES / SECURITY QUESTIONS:

SITE NAME: | URL:
USERNAME: | PASSWORD:
EMAIL ADDRESS:
NOTES / SECURITY QUESTIONS:

SITE NAME: | URL:
USERNAME: | PASSWORD:
EMAIL ADDRESS:
NOTES / SECURITY QUESTIONS:

B

SITE NAME:	URL:
USERNAME:	PASSWORD:
EMAIL ADDRESS:	
NOTES / SECURITY QUESTIONS:	

SITE NAME:	URL:
USERNAME:	PASSWORD:
EMAIL ADDRESS:	
NOTES / SECURITY QUESTIONS:	

SITE NAME:	URL:
USERNAME:	PASSWORD:
EMAIL ADDRESS:	
NOTES / SECURITY QUESTIONS:	

SITE NAME:	URL:
USERNAME:	PASSWORD:
EMAIL ADDRESS:	
NOTES / SECURITY QUESTIONS:	

B

SITE NAME:	URL:
USERNAME:	PASSWORD:
EMAIL ADDRESS:	
NOTES / SECURITY QUESTIONS:	

SITE NAME:	URL:
USERNAME:	PASSWORD:
EMAIL ADDRESS:	
NOTES / SECURITY QUESTIONS:	

SITE NAME:	URL:
USERNAME:	PASSWORD:
EMAIL ADDRESS:	
NOTES / SECURITY QUESTIONS:	

SITE NAME:	URL:
USERNAME:	PASSWORD:
EMAIL ADDRESS:	
NOTES / SECURITY QUESTIONS:	

C

SITE NAME:	URL:
USERNAME:	PASSWORD:
EMAIL ADDRESS:	
NOTES / SECURITY QUESTIONS:	

SITE NAME:	URL:
USERNAME:	PASSWORD:
EMAIL ADDRESS:	
NOTES / SECURITY QUESTIONS:	

SITE NAME:	URL:
USERNAME:	PASSWORD:
EMAIL ADDRESS:	
NOTES / SECURITY QUESTIONS:	

SITE NAME:	URL:
USERNAME:	PASSWORD:
EMAIL ADDRESS:	
NOTES / SECURITY QUESTIONS:	

C

SITE NAME:	URL:
USERNAME:	PASSWORD:
EMAIL ADDRESS:	
NOTES / SECURITY QUESTIONS:	

SITE NAME:	URL:
USERNAME:	PASSWORD:
EMAIL ADDRESS:	
NOTES / SECURITY QUESTIONS:	

SITE NAME:	URL:
USERNAME:	PASSWORD:
EMAIL ADDRESS:	
NOTES / SECURITY QUESTIONS:	

SITE NAME:	URL:
USERNAME:	PASSWORD:
EMAIL ADDRESS:	
NOTES / SECURITY QUESTIONS:	

C

SITE NAME:	URL:
USERNAME:	PASSWORD:
EMAIL ADDRESS:	
NOTES / SECURITY QUESTIONS:	

SITE NAME:	URL:
USERNAME:	PASSWORD:
EMAIL ADDRESS:	
NOTES / SECURITY QUESTIONS:	

SITE NAME:	URL:
USERNAME:	PASSWORD:
EMAIL ADDRESS:	
NOTES / SECURITY QUESTIONS:	

SITE NAME:	URL:
USERNAME:	PASSWORD:
EMAIL ADDRESS:	
NOTES / SECURITY QUESTIONS:	

C

SITE NAME:	URL:
USERNAME:	PASSWORD:
EMAIL ADDRESS:	
NOTES / SECURITY QUESTIONS:	

SITE NAME:	URL:
USERNAME:	PASSWORD:
EMAIL ADDRESS:	
NOTES / SECURITY QUESTIONS:	

SITE NAME:	URL:
USERNAME:	PASSWORD:
EMAIL ADDRESS:	
NOTES / SECURITY QUESTIONS:	

SITE NAME:	URL:
USERNAME:	PASSWORD:
EMAIL ADDRESS:	
NOTES / SECURITY QUESTIONS:	

D

SITE NAME:	URL:
USERNAME:	PASSWORD:
EMAIL ADDRESS:	
NOTES / SECURITY QUESTIONS:	

SITE NAME:	URL:
USERNAME:	PASSWORD:
EMAIL ADDRESS:	
NOTES / SECURITY QUESTIONS:	

SITE NAME:	URL:
USERNAME:	PASSWORD:
EMAIL ADDRESS:	
NOTES / SECURITY QUESTIONS:	

SITE NAME:	URL:
USERNAME:	PASSWORD:
EMAIL ADDRESS:	
NOTES / SECURITY QUESTIONS:	

D

SITE NAME:	URL:
USERNAME:	PASSWORD:
EMAIL ADDRESS:	
NOTES / SECURITY QUESTIONS:	

SITE NAME:	URL:
USERNAME:	PASSWORD:
EMAIL ADDRESS:	
NOTES / SECURITY QUESTIONS:	

SITE NAME:	URL:
USERNAME:	PASSWORD:
EMAIL ADDRESS:	
NOTES / SECURITY QUESTIONS:	

SITE NAME:	URL:
USERNAME:	PASSWORD:
EMAIL ADDRESS:	
NOTES / SECURITY QUESTIONS:	

D

SITE NAME:	URL:
USERNAME:	PASSWORD:
EMAIL ADDRESS:	
NOTES / SECURITY QUESTIONS:	

SITE NAME:	URL:
USERNAME:	PASSWORD:
EMAIL ADDRESS:	
NOTES / SECURITY QUESTIONS:	

SITE NAME:	URL:
USERNAME:	PASSWORD:
EMAIL ADDRESS:	
NOTES / SECURITY QUESTIONS:	

SITE NAME:	URL:
USERNAME:	PASSWORD:
EMAIL ADDRESS:	
NOTES / SECURITY QUESTIONS:	

D

SITE NAME:	URL:
USERNAME:	PASSWORD:
EMAIL ADDRESS:	
NOTES / SECURITY QUESTIONS:	

SITE NAME:	URL:
USERNAME:	PASSWORD:
EMAIL ADDRESS:	
NOTES / SECURITY QUESTIONS:	

SITE NAME:	URL:
USERNAME:	PASSWORD:
EMAIL ADDRESS:	
NOTES / SECURITY QUESTIONS:	

SITE NAME:	URL:
USERNAME:	PASSWORD:
EMAIL ADDRESS:	
NOTES / SECURITY QUESTIONS:	

E

SITE NAME:	URL:
USERNAME:	PASSWORD:
EMAIL ADDRESS:	
NOTES / SECURITY QUESTIONS:	

SITE NAME:	URL:
USERNAME:	PASSWORD:
EMAIL ADDRESS:	
NOTES / SECURITY QUESTIONS:	

SITE NAME:	URL:
USERNAME:	PASSWORD:
EMAIL ADDRESS:	
NOTES / SECURITY QUESTIONS:	

SITE NAME:	URL:
USERNAME:	PASSWORD:
EMAIL ADDRESS:	
NOTES / SECURITY QUESTIONS:	

E

SITE NAME:	URL:
USERNAME:	PASSWORD:
EMAIL ADDRESS:	
NOTES / SECURITY QUESTIONS:	

SITE NAME:	URL:
USERNAME:	PASSWORD:
EMAIL ADDRESS:	
NOTES / SECURITY QUESTIONS:	

SITE NAME:	URL:
USERNAME:	PASSWORD:
EMAIL ADDRESS:	
NOTES / SECURITY QUESTIONS:	

SITE NAME:	URL:
USERNAME:	PASSWORD:
EMAIL ADDRESS:	
NOTES / SECURITY QUESTIONS:	

E

SITE NAME:	URL:
USERNAME:	PASSWORD:
EMAIL ADDRESS:	
NOTES / SECURITY QUESTIONS:	

SITE NAME:	URL:
USERNAME:	PASSWORD:
EMAIL ADDRESS:	
NOTES / SECURITY QUESTIONS:	

SITE NAME:	URL:
USERNAME:	PASSWORD:
EMAIL ADDRESS:	
NOTES / SECURITY QUESTIONS:	

SITE NAME:	URL:
USERNAME:	PASSWORD:
EMAIL ADDRESS:	
NOTES / SECURITY QUESTIONS:	

E

SITE NAME:	URL:
USERNAME:	PASSWORD:
EMAIL ADDRESS:	
NOTES / SECURITY QUESTIONS:	

SITE NAME:	URL:
USERNAME:	PASSWORD:
EMAIL ADDRESS:	
NOTES / SECURITY QUESTIONS:	

SITE NAME:	URL:
USERNAME:	PASSWORD:
EMAIL ADDRESS:	
NOTES / SECURITY QUESTIONS:	

SITE NAME:	URL:
USERNAME:	PASSWORD:
EMAIL ADDRESS:	
NOTES / SECURITY QUESTIONS:	

F

SITE NAME:	URL:
USERNAME:	PASSWORD:
EMAIL ADDRESS:	
NOTES / SECURITY QUESTIONS:	

SITE NAME:	URL:
USERNAME:	PASSWORD:
EMAIL ADDRESS:	
NOTES / SECURITY QUESTIONS:	

SITE NAME:	URL:
USERNAME:	PASSWORD:
EMAIL ADDRESS:	
NOTES / SECURITY QUESTIONS:	

SITE NAME:	URL:
USERNAME:	PASSWORD:
EMAIL ADDRESS:	
NOTES / SECURITY QUESTIONS:	

F

SITE NAME:
URL:
USERNAME:
PASSWORD:
EMAIL ADDRESS:
NOTES / SECURITY QUESTIONS:

SITE NAME:
URL:
USERNAME:
PASSWORD:
EMAIL ADDRESS:
NOTES / SECURITY QUESTIONS:

SITE NAME:
URL:
USERNAME:
PASSWORD:
EMAIL ADDRESS:
NOTES / SECURITY QUESTIONS:

SITE NAME:
URL:
USERNAME:
PASSWORD:
EMAIL ADDRESS:
NOTES / SECURITY QUESTIONS:

F

SITE NAME:	URL:
USERNAME:	PASSWORD:
EMAIL ADDRESS:	
NOTES / SECURITY QUESTIONS:	

SITE NAME:	URL:
USERNAME:	PASSWORD:
EMAIL ADDRESS:	
NOTES / SECURITY QUESTIONS:	

SITE NAME:	URL:
USERNAME:	PASSWORD:
EMAIL ADDRESS:	
NOTES / SECURITY QUESTIONS:	

SITE NAME:	URL:
USERNAME:	PASSWORD:
EMAIL ADDRESS:	
NOTES / SECURITY QUESTIONS:	

F

SITE NAME:	URL:
USERNAME:	PASSWORD:
EMAIL ADDRESS:	
NOTES / SECURITY QUESTIONS:	

SITE NAME:	URL:
USERNAME:	PASSWORD:
EMAIL ADDRESS:	
NOTES / SECURITY QUESTIONS:	

SITE NAME:	URL:
USERNAME:	PASSWORD:
EMAIL ADDRESS:	
NOTES / SECURITY QUESTIONS:	

SITE NAME:	URL:
USERNAME:	PASSWORD:
EMAIL ADDRESS:	
NOTES / SECURITY QUESTIONS:	

G

SITE NAME:	URL:
USERNAME:	PASSWORD:
EMAIL ADDRESS:	
NOTES / SECURITY QUESTIONS:	

SITE NAME:	URL:
USERNAME:	PASSWORD:
EMAIL ADDRESS:	
NOTES / SECURITY QUESTIONS:	

SITE NAME:	URL:
USERNAME:	PASSWORD:
EMAIL ADDRESS:	
NOTES / SECURITY QUESTIONS:	

SITE NAME:	URL:
USERNAME:	PASSWORD:
EMAIL ADDRESS:	
NOTES / SECURITY QUESTIONS:	

G

SITE NAME:	URL:
USERNAME:	PASSWORD:
EMAIL ADDRESS:	
NOTES / SECURITY QUESTIONS:	

SITE NAME:	URL:
USERNAME:	PASSWORD:
EMAIL ADDRESS:	
NOTES / SECURITY QUESTIONS:	

SITE NAME:	URL:
USERNAME:	PASSWORD:
EMAIL ADDRESS:	
NOTES / SECURITY QUESTIONS:	

SITE NAME:	URL:
USERNAME:	PASSWORD:
EMAIL ADDRESS:	
NOTES / SECURITY QUESTIONS:	

G

SITE NAME:	URL:
USERNAME:	PASSWORD:
EMAIL ADDRESS:	
NOTES / SECURITY QUESTIONS:	

SITE NAME:	URL:
USERNAME:	PASSWORD:
EMAIL ADDRESS:	
NOTES / SECURITY QUESTIONS:	

SITE NAME:	URL:
USERNAME:	PASSWORD:
EMAIL ADDRESS:	
NOTES / SECURITY QUESTIONS:	

SITE NAME:	URL:
USERNAME:	PASSWORD:
EMAIL ADDRESS:	
NOTES / SECURITY QUESTIONS:	

G

SITE NAME:	URL:
USERNAME:	PASSWORD:
EMAIL ADDRESS:	
NOTES / SECURITY QUESTIONS:	

SITE NAME:	URL:
USERNAME:	PASSWORD:
EMAIL ADDRESS:	
NOTES / SECURITY QUESTIONS:	

SITE NAME:	URL:
USERNAME:	PASSWORD:
EMAIL ADDRESS:	
NOTES / SECURITY QUESTIONS:	

SITE NAME:	URL:
USERNAME:	PASSWORD:
EMAIL ADDRESS:	
NOTES / SECURITY QUESTIONS:	

H

SITE NAME:	URL:
USERNAME:	PASSWORD:
EMAIL ADDRESS:	
NOTES / SECURITY QUESTIONS:	
SITE NAME:	URL:
USERNAME:	PASSWORD:
EMAIL ADDRESS:	
NOTES / SECURITY QUESTIONS:	
SITE NAME:	URL:
USERNAME:	PASSWORD:
EMAIL ADDRESS:	
NOTES / SECURITY QUESTIONS:	
SITE NAME:	URL:
USERNAME:	PASSWORD:
EMAIL ADDRESS:	
NOTES / SECURITY QUESTIONS:	

H

SITE NAME:	URL:
USERNAME:	PASSWORD:
EMAIL ADDRESS:	
NOTES / SECURITY QUESTIONS:	

SITE NAME:	URL:
USERNAME:	PASSWORD:
EMAIL ADDRESS:	
NOTES / SECURITY QUESTIONS:	

SITE NAME:	URL:
USERNAME:	PASSWORD:
EMAIL ADDRESS:	
NOTES / SECURITY QUESTIONS:	

SITE NAME:	URL:
USERNAME:	PASSWORD:
EMAIL ADDRESS:	
NOTES / SECURITY QUESTIONS:	

H

SITE NAME:	URL:
USERNAME:	PASSWORD:
EMAIL ADDRESS:	
NOTES / SECURITY QUESTIONS:	

SITE NAME:	URL:
USERNAME:	PASSWORD:
EMAIL ADDRESS:	
NOTES / SECURITY QUESTIONS:	

SITE NAME:	URL:
USERNAME:	PASSWORD:
EMAIL ADDRESS:	
NOTES / SECURITY QUESTIONS:	

SITE NAME:	URL:
USERNAME:	PASSWORD:
EMAIL ADDRESS:	
NOTES / SECURITY QUESTIONS:	

H

SITE NAME:	URL:
USERNAME:	PASSWORD:
EMAIL ADDRESS:	
NOTES / SECURITY QUESTIONS:	

SITE NAME:	URL:
USERNAME:	PASSWORD:
EMAIL ADDRESS:	
NOTES / SECURITY QUESTIONS:	

SITE NAME:	URL:
USERNAME:	PASSWORD:
EMAIL ADDRESS:	
NOTES / SECURITY QUESTIONS:	

SITE NAME:	URL:
USERNAME:	PASSWORD:
EMAIL ADDRESS:	
NOTES / SECURITY QUESTIONS:	

SITE NAME:	URL:
USERNAME:	PASSWORD:
EMAIL ADDRESS:	
NOTES / SECURITY QUESTIONS:	

SITE NAME:	URL:
USERNAME:	PASSWORD:
EMAIL ADDRESS:	
NOTES / SECURITY QUESTIONS:	

SITE NAME:	URL:
USERNAME:	PASSWORD:
EMAIL ADDRESS:	
NOTES / SECURITY QUESTIONS:	

SITE NAME:	URL:
USERNAME:	PASSWORD:
EMAIL ADDRESS:	
NOTES / SECURITY QUESTIONS:	

SITE NAME:	URL:
USERNAME:	PASSWORD:
EMAIL ADDRESS:	
NOTES / SECURITY QUESTIONS:	

SITE NAME:	URL:
USERNAME:	PASSWORD:
EMAIL ADDRESS:	
NOTES / SECURITY QUESTIONS:	

SITE NAME:	URL:
USERNAME:	PASSWORD:
EMAIL ADDRESS:	
NOTES / SECURITY QUESTIONS:	

SITE NAME:	URL:
USERNAME:	PASSWORD:
EMAIL ADDRESS:	
NOTES / SECURITY QUESTIONS:	

SITE NAME:	URL:
USERNAME:	PASSWORD:
EMAIL ADDRESS:	
NOTES / SECURITY QUESTIONS:	

SITE NAME:	URL:
USERNAME:	PASSWORD:
EMAIL ADDRESS:	
NOTES / SECURITY QUESTIONS:	

SITE NAME:	URL:
USERNAME:	PASSWORD:
EMAIL ADDRESS:	
NOTES / SECURITY QUESTIONS:	

SITE NAME:	URL:
USERNAME:	PASSWORD:
EMAIL ADDRESS:	
NOTES / SECURITY QUESTIONS:	

SITE NAME:	URL:
USERNAME:	PASSWORD:
EMAIL ADDRESS:	
NOTES / SECURITY QUESTIONS:	

SITE NAME:	URL:
USERNAME:	PASSWORD:
EMAIL ADDRESS:	
NOTES / SECURITY QUESTIONS:	

SITE NAME:	URL:
USERNAME:	PASSWORD:
EMAIL ADDRESS:	
NOTES / SECURITY QUESTIONS:	

SITE NAME:	URL:
USERNAME:	PASSWORD:
EMAIL ADDRESS:	
NOTES / SECURITY QUESTIONS:	

J

SITE NAME:	URL:
USERNAME:	PASSWORD:
EMAIL ADDRESS:	
NOTES / SECURITY QUESTIONS:	

SITE NAME:	URL:
USERNAME:	PASSWORD:
EMAIL ADDRESS:	
NOTES / SECURITY QUESTIONS:	

SITE NAME:	URL:
USERNAME:	PASSWORD:
EMAIL ADDRESS:	
NOTES / SECURITY QUESTIONS:	

SITE NAME:	URL:
USERNAME:	PASSWORD:
EMAIL ADDRESS:	
NOTES / SECURITY QUESTIONS:	

J

SITE NAME:	URL:
USERNAME:	PASSWORD:
EMAIL ADDRESS:	
NOTES / SECURITY QUESTIONS:	

SITE NAME:	URL:
USERNAME:	PASSWORD:
EMAIL ADDRESS:	
NOTES / SECURITY QUESTIONS:	

SITE NAME:	URL:
USERNAME:	PASSWORD:
EMAIL ADDRESS:	
NOTES / SECURITY QUESTIONS:	

SITE NAME:	URL:
USERNAME:	PASSWORD:
EMAIL ADDRESS:	
NOTES / SECURITY QUESTIONS:	

J

SITE NAME:	URL:
USERNAME:	PASSWORD:
EMAIL ADDRESS:	
NOTES / SECURITY QUESTIONS:	

SITE NAME:	URL:
USERNAME:	PASSWORD:
EMAIL ADDRESS:	
NOTES / SECURITY QUESTIONS:	

SITE NAME:	URL:
USERNAME:	PASSWORD:
EMAIL ADDRESS:	
NOTES / SECURITY QUESTIONS:	

SITE NAME:	URL:
USERNAME:	PASSWORD:
EMAIL ADDRESS:	
NOTES / SECURITY QUESTIONS:	

J

SITE NAME:	URL:
USERNAME:	PASSWORD:
EMAIL ADDRESS:	
NOTES / SECURITY QUESTIONS:	

SITE NAME:	URL:
USERNAME:	PASSWORD:
EMAIL ADDRESS:	
NOTES / SECURITY QUESTIONS:	

SITE NAME:	URL:
USERNAME:	PASSWORD:
EMAIL ADDRESS:	
NOTES / SECURITY QUESTIONS:	

SITE NAME:	URL:
USERNAME:	PASSWORD:
EMAIL ADDRESS:	
NOTES / SECURITY QUESTIONS:	

K

SITE NAME:	URL:
USERNAME:	PASSWORD:
EMAIL ADDRESS:	
NOTES / SECURITY QUESTIONS:	

SITE NAME:	URL:
USERNAME:	PASSWORD:
EMAIL ADDRESS:	
NOTES / SECURITY QUESTIONS:	

SITE NAME:	URL:
USERNAME:	PASSWORD:
EMAIL ADDRESS:	
NOTES / SECURITY QUESTIONS:	

SITE NAME:	URL:
USERNAME:	PASSWORD:
EMAIL ADDRESS:	
NOTES / SECURITY QUESTIONS:	

K

SITE NAME:	URL:
USERNAME:	PASSWORD:
EMAIL ADDRESS:	
NOTES / SECURITY QUESTIONS:	

SITE NAME:	URL:
USERNAME:	PASSWORD:
EMAIL ADDRESS:	
NOTES / SECURITY QUESTIONS:	

SITE NAME:	URL:
USERNAME:	PASSWORD:
EMAIL ADDRESS:	
NOTES / SECURITY QUESTIONS:	

SITE NAME:	URL:
USERNAME:	PASSWORD:
EMAIL ADDRESS:	
NOTES / SECURITY QUESTIONS:	

K

SITE NAME:	URL:
USERNAME:	PASSWORD:
EMAIL ADDRESS:	
NOTES / SECURITY QUESTIONS:	

SITE NAME:	URL:
USERNAME:	PASSWORD:
EMAIL ADDRESS:	
NOTES / SECURITY QUESTIONS:	

SITE NAME:	URL:
USERNAME:	PASSWORD:
EMAIL ADDRESS:	
NOTES / SECURITY QUESTIONS:	

SITE NAME:	URL:
USERNAME:	PASSWORD:
EMAIL ADDRESS:	
NOTES / SECURITY QUESTIONS:	

K

SITE NAME:	URL:
USERNAME:	PASSWORD:
EMAIL ADDRESS:	
NOTES / SECURITY QUESTIONS:	

SITE NAME:	URL:
USERNAME:	PASSWORD:
EMAIL ADDRESS:	
NOTES / SECURITY QUESTIONS:	

SITE NAME:	URL:
USERNAME:	PASSWORD:
EMAIL ADDRESS:	
NOTES / SECURITY QUESTIONS:	

SITE NAME:	URL:
USERNAME:	PASSWORD:
EMAIL ADDRESS:	
NOTES / SECURITY QUESTIONS:	

L

SITE NAME:	URL:
USERNAME:	PASSWORD:
EMAIL ADDRESS:	
NOTES / SECURITY QUESTIONS:	

SITE NAME:	URL:
USERNAME:	PASSWORD:
EMAIL ADDRESS:	
NOTES / SECURITY QUESTIONS:	

SITE NAME:	URL:
USERNAME:	PASSWORD:
EMAIL ADDRESS:	
NOTES / SECURITY QUESTIONS:	

SITE NAME:	URL:
USERNAME:	PASSWORD:
EMAIL ADDRESS:	
NOTES / SECURITY QUESTIONS:	

L

SITE NAME:	URL:
USERNAME:	PASSWORD:
EMAIL ADDRESS:	
NOTES / SECURITY QUESTIONS:	

SITE NAME:	URL:
USERNAME:	PASSWORD:
EMAIL ADDRESS:	
NOTES / SECURITY QUESTIONS:	

SITE NAME:	URL:
USERNAME:	PASSWORD:
EMAIL ADDRESS:	
NOTES / SECURITY QUESTIONS:	

SITE NAME:	URL:
USERNAME:	PASSWORD:
EMAIL ADDRESS:	
NOTES / SECURITY QUESTIONS:	

L

SITE NAME:
URL:
USERNAME:
PASSWORD:
EMAIL ADDRESS:
NOTES / SECURITY QUESTIONS:

SITE NAME:
URL:
USERNAME:
PASSWORD:
EMAIL ADDRESS:
NOTES / SECURITY QUESTIONS:

SITE NAME:
URL:
USERNAME:
PASSWORD:
EMAIL ADDRESS:
NOTES / SECURITY QUESTIONS:

SITE NAME:
URL:
USERNAME:
PASSWORD:
EMAIL ADDRESS:
NOTES / SECURITY QUESTIONS:

L

SITE NAME:	URL:
USERNAME:	PASSWORD:
EMAIL ADDRESS:	
NOTES / SECURITY QUESTIONS:	

SITE NAME:	URL:
USERNAME:	PASSWORD:
EMAIL ADDRESS:	
NOTES / SECURITY QUESTIONS:	

SITE NAME:	URL:
USERNAME:	PASSWORD:
EMAIL ADDRESS:	
NOTES / SECURITY QUESTIONS:	

SITE NAME:	URL:
USERNAME:	PASSWORD:
EMAIL ADDRESS:	
NOTES / SECURITY QUESTIONS:	

M

SITE NAME:	URL:
USERNAME:	PASSWORD:
EMAIL ADDRESS:	
NOTES / SECURITY QUESTIONS:	

SITE NAME:	URL:
USERNAME:	PASSWORD:
EMAIL ADDRESS:	
NOTES / SECURITY QUESTIONS:	

SITE NAME:	URL:
USERNAME:	PASSWORD:
EMAIL ADDRESS:	
NOTES / SECURITY QUESTIONS:	

SITE NAME:	URL:
USERNAME:	PASSWORD:
EMAIL ADDRESS:	
NOTES / SECURITY QUESTIONS:	

M

SITE NAME:	URL:
USERNAME:	PASSWORD:

EMAIL ADDRESS:

NOTES / SECURITY QUESTIONS:

SITE NAME:	URL:
USERNAME:	PASSWORD:

EMAIL ADDRESS:

NOTES / SECURITY QUESTIONS:

SITE NAME:	URL:
USERNAME:	PASSWORD:

EMAIL ADDRESS:

NOTES / SECURITY QUESTIONS:

SITE NAME:	URL:
USERNAME:	PASSWORD:

EMAIL ADDRESS:

NOTES / SECURITY QUESTIONS:

M

SITE NAME:	URL:
USERNAME:	PASSWORD:
EMAIL ADDRESS:	
NOTES / SECURITY QUESTIONS:	

SITE NAME:	URL:
USERNAME:	PASSWORD:
EMAIL ADDRESS:	
NOTES / SECURITY QUESTIONS:	

SITE NAME:	URL:
USERNAME:	PASSWORD:
EMAIL ADDRESS:	
NOTES / SECURITY QUESTIONS:	

SITE NAME:	URL:
USERNAME:	PASSWORD:
EMAIL ADDRESS:	
NOTES / SECURITY QUESTIONS:	

M

SITE NAME:	URL:
USERNAME:	PASSWORD:
EMAIL ADDRESS:	
NOTES / SECURITY QUESTIONS:	

SITE NAME:	URL:
USERNAME:	PASSWORD:
EMAIL ADDRESS:	
NOTES / SECURITY QUESTIONS:	

SITE NAME:	URL:
USERNAME:	PASSWORD:
EMAIL ADDRESS:	
NOTES / SECURITY QUESTIONS:	

SITE NAME:	URL:
USERNAME:	PASSWORD:
EMAIL ADDRESS:	
NOTES / SECURITY QUESTIONS:	

N

SITE NAME:	URL:
USERNAME:	PASSWORD:
EMAIL ADDRESS:	
NOTES / SECURITY QUESTIONS:	

SITE NAME:	URL:
USERNAME:	PASSWORD:
EMAIL ADDRESS:	
NOTES / SECURITY QUESTIONS:	

SITE NAME:	URL:
USERNAME:	PASSWORD:
EMAIL ADDRESS:	
NOTES / SECURITY QUESTIONS:	

SITE NAME:	URL:
USERNAME:	PASSWORD:
EMAIL ADDRESS:	
NOTES / SECURITY QUESTIONS:	

N

SITE NAME:	URL:
USERNAME:	PASSWORD:
EMAIL ADDRESS:	
NOTES / SECURITY QUESTIONS:	

SITE NAME:	URL:
USERNAME:	PASSWORD:
EMAIL ADDRESS:	
NOTES / SECURITY QUESTIONS:	

SITE NAME:	URL:
USERNAME:	PASSWORD:
EMAIL ADDRESS:	
NOTES / SECURITY QUESTIONS:	

SITE NAME:	URL:
USERNAME:	PASSWORD:
EMAIL ADDRESS:	
NOTES / SECURITY QUESTIONS:	

N

SITE NAME:	URL:
USERNAME:	PASSWORD:
EMAIL ADDRESS:	
NOTES / SECURITY QUESTIONS:	

SITE NAME:	URL:
USERNAME:	PASSWORD:
EMAIL ADDRESS:	
NOTES / SECURITY QUESTIONS:	

SITE NAME:	URL:
USERNAME:	PASSWORD:
EMAIL ADDRESS:	
NOTES / SECURITY QUESTIONS:	

SITE NAME:	URL:
USERNAME:	PASSWORD:
EMAIL ADDRESS:	
NOTES / SECURITY QUESTIONS:	

N

SITE NAME:	URL:
USERNAME:	PASSWORD:
EMAIL ADDRESS:	
NOTES / SECURITY QUESTIONS:	

SITE NAME:	URL:
USERNAME:	PASSWORD:
EMAIL ADDRESS:	
NOTES / SECURITY QUESTIONS:	

SITE NAME:	URL:
USERNAME:	PASSWORD:
EMAIL ADDRESS:	
NOTES / SECURITY QUESTIONS:	

SITE NAME:	URL:
USERNAME:	PASSWORD:
EMAIL ADDRESS:	
NOTES / SECURITY QUESTIONS:	

O

SITE NAME:	URL:
USERNAME:	PASSWORD:

EMAIL ADDRESS:

NOTES / SECURITY QUESTIONS:

SITE NAME:	URL:
USERNAME:	PASSWORD:

EMAIL ADDRESS:

NOTES / SECURITY QUESTIONS:

SITE NAME:	URL:
USERNAME:	PASSWORD:

EMAIL ADDRESS:

NOTES / SECURITY QUESTIONS:

SITE NAME:	URL:
USERNAME:	PASSWORD:

EMAIL ADDRESS:

NOTES / SECURITY QUESTIONS:

O

SITE NAME:	URL:
USERNAME:	PASSWORD:
EMAIL ADDRESS:	
NOTES / SECURITY QUESTIONS:	

SITE NAME:	URL:
USERNAME:	PASSWORD:
EMAIL ADDRESS:	
NOTES / SECURITY QUESTIONS:	

SITE NAME:	URL:
USERNAME:	PASSWORD:
EMAIL ADDRESS:	
NOTES / SECURITY QUESTIONS:	

SITE NAME:	URL:
USERNAME:	PASSWORD:
EMAIL ADDRESS:	
NOTES / SECURITY QUESTIONS:	

O

SITE NAME:	URL:
USERNAME:	PASSWORD:
EMAIL ADDRESS:	
NOTES / SECURITY QUESTIONS:	

SITE NAME:	URL:
USERNAME:	PASSWORD:
EMAIL ADDRESS:	
NOTES / SECURITY QUESTIONS:	

SITE NAME:	URL:
USERNAME:	PASSWORD:
EMAIL ADDRESS:	
NOTES / SECURITY QUESTIONS:	

SITE NAME:	URL:
USERNAME:	PASSWORD:
EMAIL ADDRESS:	
NOTES / SECURITY QUESTIONS:	

O

SITE NAME:

URL:

USERNAME:

PASSWORD:

EMAIL ADDRESS:

NOTES / SECURITY QUESTIONS:

SITE NAME:

URL:

USERNAME:

PASSWORD:

EMAIL ADDRESS:

NOTES / SECURITY QUESTIONS:

SITE NAME:

URL:

USERNAME:

PASSWORD:

EMAIL ADDRESS:

NOTES / SECURITY QUESTIONS:

SITE NAME:

URL:

USERNAME:

PASSWORD:

EMAIL ADDRESS:

NOTES / SECURITY QUESTIONS:

P

SITE NAME:	URL:
USERNAME:	PASSWORD:
EMAIL ADDRESS:	
NOTES / SECURITY QUESTIONS:	

SITE NAME:	URL:
USERNAME:	PASSWORD:
EMAIL ADDRESS:	
NOTES / SECURITY QUESTIONS:	

SITE NAME:	URL:
USERNAME:	PASSWORD:
EMAIL ADDRESS:	
NOTES / SECURITY QUESTIONS:	

SITE NAME:	URL:
USERNAME:	PASSWORD:
EMAIL ADDRESS:	
NOTES / SECURITY QUESTIONS:	

P

SITE NAME:	URL:
USERNAME:	PASSWORD:
EMAIL ADDRESS:	
NOTES / SECURITY QUESTIONS:	

SITE NAME:	URL:
USERNAME:	PASSWORD:
EMAIL ADDRESS:	
NOTES / SECURITY QUESTIONS:	

SITE NAME:	URL:
USERNAME:	PASSWORD:
EMAIL ADDRESS:	
NOTES / SECURITY QUESTIONS:	

SITE NAME:	URL:
USERNAME:	PASSWORD:
EMAIL ADDRESS:	
NOTES / SECURITY QUESTIONS:	

P

SITE NAME:	URL:
USERNAME:	PASSWORD:
EMAIL ADDRESS:	
NOTES / SECURITY QUESTIONS:	

SITE NAME:	URL:
USERNAME:	PASSWORD:
EMAIL ADDRESS:	
NOTES / SECURITY QUESTIONS:	

SITE NAME:	URL:
USERNAME:	PASSWORD:
EMAIL ADDRESS:	
NOTES / SECURITY QUESTIONS:	

SITE NAME:	URL:
USERNAME:	PASSWORD:
EMAIL ADDRESS:	
NOTES / SECURITY QUESTIONS:	

P

SITE NAME:	URL:
USERNAME:	PASSWORD:
EMAIL ADDRESS:	
NOTES / SECURITY QUESTIONS:	

SITE NAME:	URL:
USERNAME:	PASSWORD:
EMAIL ADDRESS:	
NOTES / SECURITY QUESTIONS:	

SITE NAME:	URL:
USERNAME:	PASSWORD:
EMAIL ADDRESS:	
NOTES / SECURITY QUESTIONS:	

SITE NAME:	URL:
USERNAME:	PASSWORD:
EMAIL ADDRESS:	
NOTES / SECURITY QUESTIONS:	

Q

SITE NAME:	URL:
USERNAME:	PASSWORD:
EMAIL ADDRESS:	
NOTES / SECURITY QUESTIONS:	

SITE NAME:	URL:
USERNAME:	PASSWORD:
EMAIL ADDRESS:	
NOTES / SECURITY QUESTIONS:	

SITE NAME:	URL:
USERNAME:	PASSWORD:
EMAIL ADDRESS:	
NOTES / SECURITY QUESTIONS:	

SITE NAME:	URL:
USERNAME:	PASSWORD:
EMAIL ADDRESS:	
NOTES / SECURITY QUESTIONS:	

Q

SITE NAME:	URL:
USERNAME:	PASSWORD:
EMAIL ADDRESS:	
NOTES / SECURITY QUESTIONS:	

SITE NAME:	URL:
USERNAME:	PASSWORD:
EMAIL ADDRESS:	
NOTES / SECURITY QUESTIONS:	

SITE NAME:	URL:
USERNAME:	PASSWORD:
EMAIL ADDRESS:	
NOTES / SECURITY QUESTIONS:	

SITE NAME:	URL:
USERNAME:	PASSWORD:
EMAIL ADDRESS:	
NOTES / SECURITY QUESTIONS:	

Q

SITE NAME:	URL:
USERNAME:	PASSWORD:
EMAIL ADDRESS:	
NOTES / SECURITY QUESTIONS:	

SITE NAME:	URL:
USERNAME:	PASSWORD:
EMAIL ADDRESS:	
NOTES / SECURITY QUESTIONS:	

SITE NAME:	URL:
USERNAME:	PASSWORD:
EMAIL ADDRESS:	
NOTES / SECURITY QUESTIONS:	

SITE NAME:	URL:
USERNAME:	PASSWORD:
EMAIL ADDRESS:	
NOTES / SECURITY QUESTIONS:	

Q

SITE NAME:	URL:
USERNAME:	PASSWORD:
EMAIL ADDRESS:	
NOTES / SECURITY QUESTIONS:	

SITE NAME:	URL:
USERNAME:	PASSWORD:
EMAIL ADDRESS:	
NOTES / SECURITY QUESTIONS:	

SITE NAME:	URL:
USERNAME:	PASSWORD:
EMAIL ADDRESS:	
NOTES / SECURITY QUESTIONS:	

SITE NAME:	URL:
USERNAME:	PASSWORD:
EMAIL ADDRESS:	
NOTES / SECURITY QUESTIONS:	

R

SITE NAME:	URL:
USERNAME:	PASSWORD:
EMAIL ADDRESS:	
NOTES / SECURITY QUESTIONS:	

SITE NAME:	URL:
USERNAME:	PASSWORD:
EMAIL ADDRESS:	
NOTES / SECURITY QUESTIONS:	

SITE NAME:	URL:
USERNAME:	PASSWORD:
EMAIL ADDRESS:	
NOTES / SECURITY QUESTIONS:	

SITE NAME:	URL:
USERNAME:	PASSWORD:
EMAIL ADDRESS:	
NOTES / SECURITY QUESTIONS:	

R

SITE NAME:	URL:
USERNAME:	PASSWORD:
EMAIL ADDRESS:	
NOTES / SECURITY QUESTIONS:	

SITE NAME:	URL:
USERNAME:	PASSWORD:
EMAIL ADDRESS:	
NOTES / SECURITY QUESTIONS:	

SITE NAME:	URL:
USERNAME:	PASSWORD:
EMAIL ADDRESS:	
NOTES / SECURITY QUESTIONS:	

SITE NAME:	URL:
USERNAME:	PASSWORD:
EMAIL ADDRESS:	
NOTES / SECURITY QUESTIONS:	

R

SITE NAME:	URL:
USERNAME:	PASSWORD:
EMAIL ADDRESS:	
NOTES / SECURITY QUESTIONS:	

SITE NAME:	URL:
USERNAME:	PASSWORD:
EMAIL ADDRESS:	
NOTES / SECURITY QUESTIONS:	

SITE NAME:	URL:
USERNAME:	PASSWORD:
EMAIL ADDRESS:	
NOTES / SECURITY QUESTIONS:	

SITE NAME:	URL:
USERNAME:	PASSWORD:
EMAIL ADDRESS:	
NOTES / SECURITY QUESTIONS:	

R

SITE NAME:	URL:
USERNAME:	PASSWORD:
EMAIL ADDRESS:	
NOTES / SECURITY QUESTIONS:	

SITE NAME:	URL:
USERNAME:	PASSWORD:
EMAIL ADDRESS:	
NOTES / SECURITY QUESTIONS:	

SITE NAME:	URL:
USERNAME:	PASSWORD:
EMAIL ADDRESS:	
NOTES / SECURITY QUESTIONS:	

SITE NAME:	URL:
USERNAME:	PASSWORD:
EMAIL ADDRESS:	
NOTES / SECURITY QUESTIONS:	

S

SITE NAME:	URL:
USERNAME:	PASSWORD:
EMAIL ADDRESS:	
NOTES / SECURITY QUESTIONS:	

SITE NAME:	URL:
USERNAME:	PASSWORD:
EMAIL ADDRESS:	
NOTES / SECURITY QUESTIONS:	

SITE NAME:	URL:
USERNAME:	PASSWORD:
EMAIL ADDRESS:	
NOTES / SECURITY QUESTIONS:	

SITE NAME:	URL:
USERNAME:	PASSWORD:
EMAIL ADDRESS:	
NOTES / SECURITY QUESTIONS:	

S

SITE NAME:	URL:
USERNAME:	PASSWORD:
EMAIL ADDRESS:	
NOTES / SECURITY QUESTIONS:	

SITE NAME:	URL:
USERNAME:	PASSWORD:
EMAIL ADDRESS:	
NOTES / SECURITY QUESTIONS:	

SITE NAME:	URL:
USERNAME:	PASSWORD:
EMAIL ADDRESS:	
NOTES / SECURITY QUESTIONS:	

SITE NAME:	URL:
USERNAME:	PASSWORD:
EMAIL ADDRESS:	
NOTES / SECURITY QUESTIONS:	

S

SITE NAME:	URL:
USERNAME:	PASSWORD:
EMAIL ADDRESS:	
NOTES / SECURITY QUESTIONS:	

SITE NAME:	URL:
USERNAME:	PASSWORD:
EMAIL ADDRESS:	
NOTES / SECURITY QUESTIONS:	

SITE NAME:	URL:
USERNAME:	PASSWORD:
EMAIL ADDRESS:	
NOTES / SECURITY QUESTIONS:	

SITE NAME:	URL:
USERNAME:	PASSWORD:
EMAIL ADDRESS:	
NOTES / SECURITY QUESTIONS:	

S

SITE NAME:	URL:
USERNAME:	PASSWORD:
EMAIL ADDRESS:	
NOTES / SECURITY QUESTIONS:	

SITE NAME:	URL:
USERNAME:	PASSWORD:
EMAIL ADDRESS:	
NOTES / SECURITY QUESTIONS:	

SITE NAME:	URL:
USERNAME:	PASSWORD:
EMAIL ADDRESS:	
NOTES / SECURITY QUESTIONS:	

SITE NAME:	URL:
USERNAME:	PASSWORD:
EMAIL ADDRESS:	
NOTES / SECURITY QUESTIONS:	

T

SITE NAME:	URL:
USERNAME:	PASSWORD:
EMAIL ADDRESS:	
NOTES / SECURITY QUESTIONS:	

SITE NAME:	URL:
USERNAME:	PASSWORD:
EMAIL ADDRESS:	
NOTES / SECURITY QUESTIONS:	

SITE NAME:	URL:
USERNAME:	PASSWORD:
EMAIL ADDRESS:	
NOTES / SECURITY QUESTIONS:	

SITE NAME:	URL:
USERNAME:	PASSWORD:
EMAIL ADDRESS:	
NOTES / SECURITY QUESTIONS:	

T

SITE NAME:	URL:
USERNAME:	PASSWORD:
EMAIL ADDRESS:	
NOTES / SECURITY QUESTIONS:	

SITE NAME:	URL:
USERNAME:	PASSWORD:
EMAIL ADDRESS:	
NOTES / SECURITY QUESTIONS:	

SITE NAME:	URL:
USERNAME:	PASSWORD:
EMAIL ADDRESS:	
NOTES / SECURITY QUESTIONS:	

SITE NAME:	URL:
USERNAME:	PASSWORD:
EMAIL ADDRESS:	
NOTES / SECURITY QUESTIONS:	

T

SITE NAME:	URL:
USERNAME:	PASSWORD:
EMAIL ADDRESS:	
NOTES / SECURITY QUESTIONS:	

SITE NAME:	URL:
USERNAME:	PASSWORD:
EMAIL ADDRESS:	
NOTES / SECURITY QUESTIONS:	

SITE NAME:	URL:
USERNAME:	PASSWORD:
EMAIL ADDRESS:	
NOTES / SECURITY QUESTIONS:	

SITE NAME:	URL:
USERNAME:	PASSWORD:
EMAIL ADDRESS:	
NOTES / SECURITY QUESTIONS:	

T

SITE NAME:	URL:
USERNAME:	PASSWORD:
EMAIL ADDRESS:	
NOTES / SECURITY QUESTIONS:	

SITE NAME:	URL:
USERNAME:	PASSWORD:
EMAIL ADDRESS:	
NOTES / SECURITY QUESTIONS:	

SITE NAME:	URL:
USERNAME:	PASSWORD:
EMAIL ADDRESS:	
NOTES / SECURITY QUESTIONS:	

SITE NAME:	URL:
USERNAME:	PASSWORD:
EMAIL ADDRESS:	
NOTES / SECURITY QUESTIONS:	

U

SITE NAME:	URL:
USERNAME:	PASSWORD:

EMAIL ADDRESS:

NOTES / SECURITY QUESTIONS:

SITE NAME:	URL:
USERNAME:	PASSWORD:

EMAIL ADDRESS:

NOTES / SECURITY QUESTIONS:

SITE NAME:	URL:
USERNAME:	PASSWORD:

EMAIL ADDRESS:

NOTES / SECURITY QUESTIONS:

SITE NAME:	URL:
USERNAME:	PASSWORD:

EMAIL ADDRESS:

NOTES / SECURITY QUESTIONS:

U

SITE NAME:	URL:
USERNAME:	PASSWORD:
EMAIL ADDRESS:	
NOTES / SECURITY QUESTIONS:	

SITE NAME:	URL:
USERNAME:	PASSWORD:
EMAIL ADDRESS:	
NOTES / SECURITY QUESTIONS:	

SITE NAME:	URL:
USERNAME:	PASSWORD:
EMAIL ADDRESS:	
NOTES / SECURITY QUESTIONS:	

SITE NAME:	URL:
USERNAME:	PASSWORD:
EMAIL ADDRESS:	
NOTES / SECURITY QUESTIONS:	

U

SITE NAME:	URL:
USERNAME:	PASSWORD:
EMAIL ADDRESS:	
NOTES / SECURITY QUESTIONS:	

SITE NAME:	URL:
USERNAME:	PASSWORD:
EMAIL ADDRESS:	
NOTES / SECURITY QUESTIONS:	

SITE NAME:	URL:
USERNAME:	PASSWORD:
EMAIL ADDRESS:	
NOTES / SECURITY QUESTIONS:	

SITE NAME:	URL:
USERNAME:	PASSWORD:
EMAIL ADDRESS:	
NOTES / SECURITY QUESTIONS:	

U

SITE NAME:	URL:
USERNAME:	PASSWORD:
EMAIL ADDRESS:	
NOTES / SECURITY QUESTIONS:	

SITE NAME:	URL:
USERNAME:	PASSWORD:
EMAIL ADDRESS:	
NOTES / SECURITY QUESTIONS:	

SITE NAME:	URL:
USERNAME:	PASSWORD:
EMAIL ADDRESS:	
NOTES / SECURITY QUESTIONS:	

SITE NAME:	URL:
USERNAME:	PASSWORD:
EMAIL ADDRESS:	
NOTES / SECURITY QUESTIONS:	

V

SITE NAME:	URL:
USERNAME:	PASSWORD:
EMAIL ADDRESS:	
NOTES / SECURITY QUESTIONS:	

SITE NAME:	URL:
USERNAME:	PASSWORD:
EMAIL ADDRESS:	
NOTES / SECURITY QUESTIONS:	

SITE NAME:	URL:
USERNAME:	PASSWORD:
EMAIL ADDRESS:	
NOTES / SECURITY QUESTIONS:	

SITE NAME:	URL:
USERNAME:	PASSWORD:
EMAIL ADDRESS:	
NOTES / SECURITY QUESTIONS:	

V

SITE NAME:	URL:
USERNAME:	PASSWORD:
EMAIL ADDRESS:	
NOTES / SECURITY QUESTIONS:	

SITE NAME:	URL:
USERNAME:	PASSWORD:
EMAIL ADDRESS:	
NOTES / SECURITY QUESTIONS:	

SITE NAME:	URL:
USERNAME:	PASSWORD:
EMAIL ADDRESS:	
NOTES / SECURITY QUESTIONS:	

SITE NAME:	URL:
USERNAME:	PASSWORD:
EMAIL ADDRESS:	
NOTES / SECURITY QUESTIONS:	

V

SITE NAME:	URL:
USERNAME:	PASSWORD:
EMAIL ADDRESS:	
NOTES / SECURITY QUESTIONS:	

SITE NAME:	URL:
USERNAME:	PASSWORD:
EMAIL ADDRESS:	
NOTES / SECURITY QUESTIONS:	

SITE NAME:	URL:
USERNAME:	PASSWORD:
EMAIL ADDRESS:	
NOTES / SECURITY QUESTIONS:	

SITE NAME:	URL:
USERNAME:	PASSWORD:
EMAIL ADDRESS:	
NOTES / SECURITY QUESTIONS:	

V

SITE NAME:	URL:
USERNAME:	PASSWORD:
EMAIL ADDRESS:	
NOTES / SECURITY QUESTIONS:	

SITE NAME:	URL:
USERNAME:	PASSWORD:
EMAIL ADDRESS:	
NOTES / SECURITY QUESTIONS:	

SITE NAME:	URL:
USERNAME:	PASSWORD:
EMAIL ADDRESS:	
NOTES / SECURITY QUESTIONS:	

SITE NAME:	URL:
USERNAME:	PASSWORD:
EMAIL ADDRESS:	
NOTES / SECURITY QUESTIONS:	

W

SITE NAME:	URL:
USERNAME:	PASSWORD:
EMAIL ADDRESS:	
NOTES / SECURITY QUESTIONS:	

SITE NAME:	URL:
USERNAME:	PASSWORD:
EMAIL ADDRESS:	
NOTES / SECURITY QUESTIONS:	

SITE NAME:	URL:
USERNAME:	PASSWORD:
EMAIL ADDRESS:	
NOTES / SECURITY QUESTIONS:	

SITE NAME:	URL:
USERNAME:	PASSWORD:
EMAIL ADDRESS:	
NOTES / SECURITY QUESTIONS:	

W

SITE NAME:	URL:
USERNAME:	PASSWORD:
EMAIL ADDRESS:	
NOTES / SECURITY QUESTIONS:	

SITE NAME:	URL:
USERNAME:	PASSWORD:
EMAIL ADDRESS:	
NOTES / SECURITY QUESTIONS:	

SITE NAME:	URL:
USERNAME:	PASSWORD:
EMAIL ADDRESS:	
NOTES / SECURITY QUESTIONS:	

SITE NAME:	URL:
USERNAME:	PASSWORD:
EMAIL ADDRESS:	
NOTES / SECURITY QUESTIONS:	

X

SITE NAME:	URL:
USERNAME:	PASSWORD:
EMAIL ADDRESS:	
NOTES / SECURITY QUESTIONS:	

SITE NAME:	URL:
USERNAME:	PASSWORD:
EMAIL ADDRESS:	
NOTES / SECURITY QUESTIONS:	

SITE NAME:	URL:
USERNAME:	PASSWORD:
EMAIL ADDRESS:	
NOTES / SECURITY QUESTIONS:	

SITE NAME:	URL:
USERNAME:	PASSWORD:
EMAIL ADDRESS:	
NOTES / SECURITY QUESTIONS:	

X

SITE NAME:	URL:
USERNAME:	PASSWORD:
EMAIL ADDRESS:	
NOTES / SECURITY QUESTIONS:	

SITE NAME:	URL:
USERNAME:	PASSWORD:
EMAIL ADDRESS:	
NOTES / SECURITY QUESTIONS:	

SITE NAME:	URL:
USERNAME:	PASSWORD:
EMAIL ADDRESS:	
NOTES / SECURITY QUESTIONS:	

SITE NAME:	URL:
USERNAME:	PASSWORD:
EMAIL ADDRESS:	
NOTES / SECURITY QUESTIONS:	

Y

SITE NAME:	URL:
USERNAME:	PASSWORD:
EMAIL ADDRESS:	
NOTES / SECURITY QUESTIONS:	

SITE NAME:	URL:
USERNAME:	PASSWORD:
EMAIL ADDRESS:	
NOTES / SECURITY QUESTIONS:	

SITE NAME:	URL:
USERNAME:	PASSWORD:
EMAIL ADDRESS:	
NOTES / SECURITY QUESTIONS:	

SITE NAME:	URL:
USERNAME:	PASSWORD:
EMAIL ADDRESS:	
NOTES / SECURITY QUESTIONS:	

Y

SITE NAME:	URL:
USERNAME:	PASSWORD:
EMAIL ADDRESS:	
NOTES / SECURITY QUESTIONS:	

SITE NAME:	URL:
USERNAME:	PASSWORD:
EMAIL ADDRESS:	
NOTES / SECURITY QUESTIONS:	

SITE NAME:	URL:
USERNAME:	PASSWORD:
EMAIL ADDRESS:	
NOTES / SECURITY QUESTIONS:	

SITE NAME:	URL:
USERNAME:	PASSWORD:
EMAIL ADDRESS:	
NOTES / SECURITY QUESTIONS:	

Z

SITE NAME:	URL:
USERNAME:	PASSWORD:
EMAIL ADDRESS:	
NOTES / SECURITY QUESTIONS:	

SITE NAME:	URL:
USERNAME:	PASSWORD:
EMAIL ADDRESS:	
NOTES / SECURITY QUESTIONS:	

SITE NAME:	URL:
USERNAME:	PASSWORD:
EMAIL ADDRESS:	
NOTES / SECURITY QUESTIONS:	

SITE NAME:	URL:
USERNAME:	PASSWORD:
EMAIL ADDRESS:	
NOTES / SECURITY QUESTIONS:	

Z

SITE NAME:	URL:
USERNAME:	PASSWORD:
EMAIL ADDRESS:	
NOTES / SECURITY QUESTIONS:	

SITE NAME:	URL:
USERNAME:	PASSWORD:
EMAIL ADDRESS:	
NOTES / SECURITY QUESTIONS:	

SITE NAME:	URL:
USERNAME:	PASSWORD:
EMAIL ADDRESS:	
NOTES / SECURITY QUESTIONS:	

SITE NAME:	URL:
USERNAME:	PASSWORD:
EMAIL ADDRESS:	
NOTES / SECURITY QUESTIONS:	

0-9

SITE NAME:	URL:
USERNAME:	PASSWORD:
EMAIL ADDRESS:	
NOTES / SECURITY QUESTIONS:	

SITE NAME:	URL:
USERNAME:	PASSWORD:
EMAIL ADDRESS:	
NOTES / SECURITY QUESTIONS:	

SITE NAME:	URL:
USERNAME:	PASSWORD:
EMAIL ADDRESS:	
NOTES / SECURITY QUESTIONS:	

SITE NAME:	URL:
USERNAME:	PASSWORD:
EMAIL ADDRESS:	
NOTES / SECURITY QUESTIONS:	

0-9

SITE NAME:	URL:
USERNAME:	PASSWORD:
EMAIL ADDRESS:	
NOTES / SECURITY QUESTIONS:	

SITE NAME:	URL:
USERNAME:	PASSWORD:
EMAIL ADDRESS:	
NOTES / SECURITY QUESTIONS:	

SITE NAME:	URL:
USERNAME:	PASSWORD:
EMAIL ADDRESS:	
NOTES / SECURITY QUESTIONS:	

SITE NAME:	URL:
USERNAME:	PASSWORD:
EMAIL ADDRESS:	
NOTES / SECURITY QUESTIONS:	

INTERNET RECORDS

EMAIL ADDRESS:	
USERNAME:	
PASSWORD:	
MAIL SERVER: POP ☐ IMAP ☐	
INCOMING MAIL:	PORT:
USERNAME:	
PASSWORD:	
OUTGOING MAIL:	PORT:
USERNAME:	
PASSWORD:	
NOTES:	

EMAIL ADDRESS:	
USERNAME:	
PASSWORD:	
MAIL SERVER: POP ☐ IMAP ☐	
INCOMING MAIL:	PORT:
USERNAME:	
PASSWORD:	
OUTGOING MAIL:	PORT:
USERNAME:	
PASSWORD:	
NOTES:	

INTERNET RECORDS

EMAIL ADDRESS:	
USERNAME:	
PASSWORD:	
MAIL SERVER: POP ☐ IMAP ☐	
INCOMING MAIL:	PORT:
USERNAME:	
PASSWORD:	
OUTGOING MAIL:	PORT:
USERNAME:	
PASSWORD:	
NOTES:	

EMAIL ADDRESS:	
USERNAME:	
PASSWORD:	
MAIL SERVER: POP ☐ IMAP ☐	
INCOMING MAIL:	PORT:
USERNAME:	
PASSWORD:	
OUTGOING MAIL:	PORT:
USERNAME:	
PASSWORD:	
NOTES:	

INTERNET RECORDS

WIFI NETWORK:
PASSWORD:
NOTES:
WIFI NETWORK:
PASSWORD:
NOTES:
WIFI NETWORK:
PASSWORD:
NOTES:
WIFI NETWORK:
PASSWORD:
NOTES:
WIFI NETWORK:
PASSWORD:
NOTES:
WIFI NETWORK:
PASSWORD:
NOTES:
WIFI NETWORK:
PASSWORD:
NOTES:

INTERNET RECORDS

WIFI NETWORK:
PASSWORD:
NOTES:
WIFI NETWORK:
PASSWORD:
NOTES:
WIFI NETWORK:
PASSWORD:
NOTES:
WIFI NETWORK:
PASSWORD:
NOTES:
WIFI NETWORK:
PASSWORD:
NOTES:
WIFI NETWORK:
PASSWORD:
NOTES:
WIFI NETWORK:
PASSWORD:
NOTES:

INTERNET RECORDS

WIFI NETWORK:
PASSWORD:
NOTES:
WIFI NETWORK:
PASSWORD:
NOTES:
WIFI NETWORK:
PASSWORD:
NOTES:
WIFI NETWORK:
PASSWORD:
NOTES:
WIFI NETWORK:
PASSWORD:
NOTES:
WIFI NETWORK:
PASSWORD:
NOTES:
WIFI NETWORK:
PASSWORD:
NOTES:

INTERNET RECORDS

WIFI NETWORK:
PASSWORD:
NOTES:
WIFI NETWORK:
PASSWORD:
NOTES:
WIFI NETWORK:
PASSWORD:
NOTES:
WIFI NETWORK:
PASSWORD:
NOTES:
WIFI NETWORK:
PASSWORD:
NOTES:
WIFI NETWORK:
PASSWORD:
NOTES:
WIFI NETWORK:
PASSWORD:
NOTES:

DATA RECORDS

PROTECTED FILE NAME:

PASSWORD / KEY:

PROTECTED FILE NAME:

PASSWORD / KEY:

PROTECTED FILE NAME:

PASSWORD / KEY:

PROTECTED FILE NAME:

PASSWORD / KEY:

PROTECTED FILE NAME:

PASSWORD / KEY:

PROTECTED FILE NAME:

PASSWORD / KEY:

PROTECTED FILE NAME:

PASSWORD / KEY:

PROTECTED FILE NAME:

PASSWORD / KEY:

PROTECTED FILE NAME:

PASSWORD / KEY:

PROTECTED FILE NAME:

PASSWORD / KEY:

PROTECTED FILE NAME:

PASSWORD KEY:

DATA RECORDS

PROTECTED FILE NAME:
PASSWORD / KEY:
PROTECTED FILE NAME:
PASSWORD / KEY:
PROTECTED FILE NAME:
PASSWORD / KEY:
PROTECTED FILE NAME:
PASSWORD / KEY:
PROTECTED FILE NAME:
PASSWORD / KEY:
PROTECTED FILE NAME:
PASSWORD / KEY:
PROTECTED FILE NAME:
PASSWORD / KEY:
PROTECTED FILE NAME:
PASSWORD / KEY:
PROTECTED FILE NAME:
PASSWORD / KEY:
PROTECTED FILE NAME:
PASSWORD / KEY:
PROTECTED FILE NAME:
PASSWORD KEY:

COMPUTER RECORDS

HOME ROUTER
WIRELESS NETWORK NAME (SSID):
WIRELESS PASSWORD:
ROUTER LOGIN URL:
LOGIN USERNAME:
LOGIN PASSWORD:
SERIAL #:
WORK ROUTER
WIRELESS NETWORK NAME (SSID):
WIRELESS PASSWORD:
ROUTER LOGIN URL:
LOGIN USERNAME:
LOGIN PASSWORD:
SERIAL #:
OTHER ROUTER
WIRELESS NETWORK NAME (SSID):
WIRELESS PASSWORD:
ROUTER LOGIN URL:
LOGIN USERNAME:
LOGIN PASSWORD:
SERIAL #:

COMPUTER RECORDS

HOME COMPUTER
BRAND / MODEL:
SERIAL #:
NOTEBOOK COMPUTER
BRAND / MODEL:
SERIAL #:
TABLET
BRAND / MODEL:
SERIAL #:
MOBILE
BRAND / MODEL:
SERIAL #:
OTHER DEVICE
BRAND / MODEL:
SERIAL #:
OTHER DEVICE
BRAND / MODEL:
SERIAL #:

COMPUTER RECORDS

OPERATING SYSTEM:

LICENSE KEY / CODE:

OPERATING SYSTEM:

LICENSE KEY / CODE:

APP NAME:

LICENSE KEY / CODE:

APP NAME:

LICENSE KEY / CODE:

APP NAME:

LICENSE KEY / CODE:

APP NAME:

LICENSE KEY / CODE:

APP NAME:

LICENSE KEY / CODE:

APP NAME:

LICENSE KEY / CODE:

APP NAME:

LICENSE KEY / CODE:

APP NAME:

LICENSE KEY / CODE:

COMPUTER RECORDS

APP NAME:
LICENSE KEY / CODE:
APP NAME:
LICENSE KEY / CODE:
APP NAME:
LICENSE KEY / CODE:
APP NAME:
LICENSE KEY / CODE:
APP NAME:
LICENSE KEY / CODE:
APP NAME:
LICENSE KEY / CODE:
APP NAME:
LICENSE KEY / CODE:
APP NAME:
LICENSE KEY / CODE:
APP NAME:
LICENSE KEY / CODE:
APP NAME:
LICENSE KEY / CODE:
APP NAME:
LICENSE KEY / CODE:

Made in the USA
Monee, IL
04 November 2026

67375794R00066